WILLISTON

Adam Seidel

BROADWAY PLAY PUBLISHING INC
New York
www.broadwayplaypub.com
info@broadwayplaypub.com

WILLISTON
© Copyright 2019 Adam Seidel

First edition: July 2019
I S B N: 978-0-88145-852-7

Book design: Marie Donovan
Page make-up: Adobe InDesign
Typeface: Palatino

A special thank you to Valentina Fratti and Miranda Theatre for believing in, and for nurturing this play.

WILLISTON received its world premiere, opening on 26 October 2018 at IATI in New York City (produced by Miranda Theatre). The cast and creative contributors were:

LARRY .... Robert LuPone
BARB...Kate Grimes
TOM..Drew Ledbetter

Director .... Valentina Fratti
Lights/set .... Graham Kindred
Sound .... Margaret Montagna
Costumes ....Matsy Stinson
Fight choreography ....Dan Renkin
Stage manager .... Ernie Fimbres
Assistant stage manager .... Aaron D van Scyoc

WILLISTON received its midwest premiere, opening on 30 May 2019 at Detroit Repertory Theatre. The cast and creative contributors were:

LARRY .... Harold Uriah Hogan
BARB.. Kelly Pino
TOM.. David Wolber

Director .... Causandra Freeman
Set design & construction .... Harry Wetzel
Lighting design .... Thomas Schraeder
Costume design .... Sandra Landfair Glover
Sound design .... Burrr Huntington
Lighting technician .... Cornell Markham
Stage manager .... Leah Smith

CHARACTERS & SETTING

TOM, *mid 40s*
BARB, *mid 40s*
LARRY, *early 60s*

The interior of a single wide trailer in a camp outside of Williston, North Dakota.

A restaurant in Williston.

Time: Spring 2013

A note on leasing reps: leasing reps negotiate with land owners on behalf of oil companies about obtaining a lease to develop the land. Leasing agents typically operate on commissions which are a percentage of the leasing price. Leasing reps are also referred to as "landmen".

Scene 1

(Day. The interior of a single wide mobile trailer fitted to look like a hotel room: two beds, a table between the beds with a phone, a small couch and a little television on a plastic stand. There's a cot folded up in the corner.)

(The one overhead light is on and the light in the bathroom is also on.)

(There's a door that leads outside and on the opposite side of the trailer, one that leads to the bathroom.)

(There's one window with semi broken blinds drawn to cover it.)

(On the wall is a paper sign attached by scotch tape. In permanent marker it says "Welcome to Williston". Next to it a smiley face.)

(We hear a car pull up outside.)

(After a moment the front door opens. We see it's light outside but grey, and there's considerable wind.)

(TOM, a man in his mid thirties, clean cut, wearing a somewhat nice looking coat and boots enters carrying a small roll on suitcase. He closes the front door quickly, and rubs his hands together to warm them up.)

(He looks around, then goes to the bathroom door and lightly knocks.)

(After no response he opens the bathroom door and looks inside. It's empty.)

(TOM *goes back to his bag, puts it on the right bed, and then sits on the bed. The mattress is unusually stiff, which he notices. He takes off his coat.*)

(*He picks up the remote for the T V and turns on the T V. The station is static.*)

(TOM *changes the channel and for a moment we hear a static-filled speech of President Obama talking about oil production in the United States.*)

(TOM *changes the channel one more time with same static result and then turns it off.*)

(TOM *goes into the bathroom, closing the door.*)

(*After a moment we hear a car pull up. Then the front door opens.* BARB, *a late forty something woman carrying a small suitcase and a to-go coffee cup, dressed in a coat and boots enters and slams the door behind her.*)

(*She looks around, sees the suitcase on the right bed and the door to the bathroom closed.*)

(*She goes to the bed and knocks* TOM'S *suitcase onto the ground, then she puts her suitcase and briefcase on the bed and sits down.*)

(*After a moment* TOM *comes out of the bathroom.* BARB *and* TOM *look at each other.*)

TOM: It's cold out there.

BARB: What?

TOM: I said, it's cold out there.

BARB: That an ice breaker or something?

TOM: When I meet someone for the first time I like to say something other than "hi".

BARB: What's wrong with "hi"?

TOM: Nothing. It's just everyone says "hi". So I try to do something a little different. And seeing as how walking from my car to the trailer I completely lost feeling in my hands I thought I'd say to you "It's cold out there."

BARB: I take it you're the new guy.

TOM: Yes. I'm Tom.

BARB: The email I got said your name was Tim.

TOM: Well it's Tom.

BARB: And you're the numbers guy?

TOM: Yep. Been left brained my whole life. Which is funny because I'm left handed.

BARB: Great.

TOM: So I didn't catch—

BARB: Barb.

TOM: Nice to meet you. That short for Barbara?

BARB: No.

TOM: Sorry.

BARB: What are you apologizing for?

TOM: I'm just getting the feeling that I'm bothering you.

BARB: You're fine. It's been a rough day.

TOM: Nothing too serious I hope.

BARB: My flight in was delayed two hours for no apparent reason other than the pilot felt the need to stand around and undress the gate agent with his eyes. Then once boarding began, said gate agent tried to bump me to tomorrow's flight.

TOM: So why didn't you get bumped?

BARB: There's two types of people in this world- those who get bumped and those who don't. Guess which I am?

TOM: I'm going to say you're the latter.

BARB: Good guess.

TOM: I was told there's going to be a third.

BARB: Larry.

TOM: Is Larry here?

BARB: Do you see Larry?

TOM: No.

BARB: Then Larry's not here yet.

TOM: I can't help but notice my stuff is on the floor.

BARB: It was on the right bed and the right bed is always mine.

TOM: Okay I'll take the left.

BARB: The left belongs to Larry.

TOM: I'll take the cot.

BARB: Nothing personal.

TOM: I get it I'm new. *(He picks up his suitcase and starts to set up the cot.)*

BARB: So before Larry arrives we should go over some things. By now I'm sure you've put it together that this will be a co-gender living situation. Up here that's how it goes and I don't like it but it is what it is. That being said there are ground rules.

TOM: Sure.

BARB: First and foremost, keep things clean. No dirty socks on the floor and don't ever piss on the toilet seat. Second, if you need to drop ass or fart or whatever you want to call it, go outside and do it far enough away from the trailer that I don't hear it. Third, this trailer is our base of operation not your pleasure palace. So no jacking off. Not in your cot, not in the shower. Got it?

TOM: About the jacking off or about everything?

BARB: Everything.

TOM: Yes. I understand.

BARB: *(Lighter.)* Good. *(She begins to unpack her clothing. She takes out a bra and some underwear and puts it on the bed.)*

TOM: Do you want me to step into the *(bathroom)*.

BARB: Why?

TOM: Your— *(underwear)*

(BARB *holds up the underwear.)*

BARB: This?

TOM: Yes.

BARB: It's just underwear, Tom. Surely you've seen it before.

TOM: I just thought that maybe you wanted some privacy.

BARB: Thank you but I'm good. But when I do start to get naked I'll give you a thirty second warning.

TOM: Great.

(BARB *begins hanging items of clothing on hangers in the closet.* TOM, *not knowing what to do, watches her. Feeling him looking at her, she re-engages in a faux friendly manner, though slightly annoyed.)*

BARB: So where you from, Tom?

TOM: I'm based out of Houston.

BARB: The way you reacted to my underwear I'd have guessed Utah.

TOM: Well I am from Denver originally.

BARB: Meaning what?

TOM: Denver is sort of close to Utah.

BARB: I wouldn't know. I've never been.

TOM: To Denver?

BARB: Yep.

TOM: You should go sometime.

BARB: I've never understood that.

TOM: What.

BARB: Whenever someone tells you where they're from and you respond that you haven't been there, their first reaction is to say you should go there.

TOM: I guess people tend to have pride about the place they are from.

BARB: Say you were from Akron. Would you tell me to go there?

TOM: I don't know. I've never been to Akron.

BARB: It's a shithole.

TOM: Well, unlike Akron, Denver is really nice.

BARB: And what makes it so?

TOM: Plenty of nature.

BARB: I'm not a fan of nature.

TOM: Lots of sunshine.

BARB: I prefer the shade.

TOM: World class skiing?

BARB: The only time I skied I broke my leg.

TOM: You know, I don't think Denver's for you.

BARB: I'm glad we're in agreement. (*She is now on her bed, looking at an iPad.*)

TOM: So the email I got mentioned you're out of the Chicago office?

BARB: Uh huh.

TOM: I've always wanted to go to Chicago.

BARB: Why?

TOM: It's a place I know nothing about.

BARB: Here's what you need to know— It's freezing for five months, then warm for two days, then freezing for another month. Then hot as shit for three straight months. Then it rains.

TOM: So what's the deal with the sign? "Welcome to Williston."

BARB: It's kind of a funny story. The first time we stayed in this camp there wasn't hot water for over a day so I went to the office and demanded to know what the hell was going on. The manager's response was "Welcome to Williston". My response was to tell him to go fuck himself. His response was to key my car. My response was to throw a rock through the office window. We've had a volatile relationship ever since.

TOM: Oh. And that was a funny story because?

BARB: I'm guessing this is your first time to Williston.

TOM: Actually it's my first time to North Dakota.

BARB: Jesus, really?

TOM: Yeah.

BARB: What do you think so far?

TOM: Granted I've only been here a little over an hour. But so far it's really interesting. The land—the way it rolls on and on. The people who live here, the way they carry themselves. Like there was this guy I drove past in town and he was just walking along with this strut. And he was wearing these boots.

BARB: People do tend to wear boots, Tom.

TOM: I just meant it feels like I've stepped back in time or something.

BARB: You have. Up until last year this town didn't get internet.

TOM: So I was hoping you could help clarify some things.

BARB: I can try.

TOM: Well, I was told that we're here to obtain a land lease.

BARB: Correct.

TOM: And the meeting is tomorrow morning but we're having a dinner with the land owner tonight?

BARB: You're doing fine so far.

TOM: So my question is, how formal will tonight be?

BARB: It's a business dinner.

TOM: True. But still, given where we are I didn't know what to wear so I brought a suit. Should I wear a suit?

BARB: Tom do you normally end every sentence with a question or is this an honor you've reserved just for me?

TOM: Sorry. It's just that this is a big opportunity for me and I don't want to screw it up.

BARB: Well we can't do a thing without Larry. So cool your jets.

(A beat)

TOM: So how long have you been with Smith? And yes I'm aware that's a question.

BARB: Fifteen years bursting with joy. How about yourself?

TOM: Just over nine months.

BARB: That's unusual.

TOM: What?

BARB: Headquarters doesn't send newbies up here anymore.

TOM: Why?

BARB: Because newbies have shown a propensity for getting eaten alive.

TOM: People I've talked with have told me this place can be rough.

BARB: It makes Detroit look like Disneyland.

TOM: Detroit five years ago or Detroit now? Cause it's really not as bad as it used to be.

(Off BARB's look:)

TOM: Point taken.

BARB: So look—I don't care that you're new or that you've never been here. All I care about is that when the chips are down, the people on my side of the table don't shit the bed. You're not a bed shitter, are you Tom?

TOM: Absolutely not.

BARB: For your sake I hope that's true. I'm going to freshen up. Give Holidays a call.

TOM: Holidays?

BARB: It's the local steak house. We need a reservation.

TOM: We don't already have one?

BARB: Holidays only lets you book reservations the day of.

TOM: What time?

BARB: Make it for six. *(Beat)* No, six thirty. *(Beat)* Actually, keep it at six.

TOM: For how many people?

BARB: We're expecting nine but make it for seven.

TOM: Why don't I just make it for nine?

BARB: Because Holidays doesn't let you book tables for more than seven people but if you show up with more they'll accommodate you. Don't ask why, it doesn't matter.

(TOM *takes out his phone.*)

TOM: I'm not getting cell reception.

BARB: Use the land line. There should be a phone book on the night stand.

TOM: So just to clarify, the reservation should be made for six o clock for seven people even though we're expecting nine.

BARB: Don't tell them that or they won't give us a table.

TOM: I won't.

BARB: Tom- this is your first task. Don't screw it up.

(BARB *exits to the bathroom.* TOM *goes to the super thin phone book on the night stand. He searches for the number, finds it, picks up the table phone and dials.*)

TOM: *(Into the phone)* Yes. I'd like to make a reservation for this evening. *(Beat)* Seven people. *(Beat)* No, just seven. *(Beat)* Do you have anything at six pm? *(Covers receiver.)* Barb?!

BARB: *(Off)* What???

TOM: They don't have anything at six!

BARB: *(Off)* Then six-thirty!!!

TOM: *(Into phone.)* How about six thirty? *(Beat)* Great. *(Beat)* Under Tom. Okay thanks. *(Hangs up.)* Alright we're good for six thirty! Barb?

BARB: *(Off)* Fantastic!!

(LARRY, *a sixty-something man in a coat carrying a small suitcase enters. He closes the front door with slam and takes in the space, totally ignoring* TOM.)

LARRY: Holy shit this has to be a mistake. They said we'd have a double wide this time. With actual rooms. And a kitchen-fucking-ette.

TOM: A kitchenette?

LARRY: It's like a kitchen. But smaller. Who are you?

TOM: Hi I'm—

LARRY: I don't care. The placement of this trailer is unacceptable fucking bullshit.

TOM: What's wrong with it?

LARRY: What's wrong with it?? It's next to the fucking road! You know how many goddamn trucks go up and down this road?

TOM: Based on your tone I'm going to say a lot.

LARRY: They never fucking stop! It's like a philharmonic of diesel engines. I mean for Christ sakes, we're important people sent here to do important shit. We need our sleep!

TOM: I understand.

LARRY: Then change our trailer!!

TOM: I can't.

LARRY: Then why are you here? And why is there a cot set up in the corner? Are we hosting borders?

TOM: The cot's for me.

LARRY: Why is the cot for you? Would someone please tell me what the hell is going on?!

TOM: I'm the numbers guy. I was sent here to help with the meeting.

LARRY: Is Barb here?

TOM: Yeah she's in the—

LARRY: *(To the bathroom)* BARB? YOU IN THERE?

TOM: Bathroom.

BARB: *(Off)* You don't have to yell! The door's made of balsa!

LARRY: Sorry Barb but I was worried. Thought maybe you got hacked up by whoever the fuck this is.

(BARB *opens the bathroom door and re-enters the main space.)*

BARB: He's the numbers guy.

LARRY: Did you know we were getting a numbers guy on this trip? Because I sure as shit didn't.

BARB: We both got an email about it beginning of the week.

LARRY: You know I don't email. If I want to contact someone I pick up the phone like a normal person and I call them.

How they treating you in Chicago?

(LARRY *and* BARB *hug hello.)*

BARB: My property taxes went up fifteen percent and the public schools are still shit. How's Minneapolis?

LARRY: Twins finished third in their division and my favorite restaurant burned down.

BARB: Good. Maybe that'll lower your cholesterol.

LARRY: I don't have high cholesterol. But speaking of cholesterol, we set for tonight at Holidays?

BARB: New guy just made reservations.

LARRY: Seven people for six P M?

TOM: Six-thirty actually.

LARRY: I haven't even been here five minutes and the guppy is already shitting the bed.

TOM: They didn't have room at six.

LARRY: Of course they have room at six! You just didn't ask the right way.

TOM: I was courteous and polite.

LARRY: Jesus Christ. *(He goes to the phone and dials a number.)* Yes hello my associate just called making reservations for tonight. *(To the room)* Under what name?

TOM: Tom.

LARRY: The name is Tom. Yeah, so we're actually gonna need a table at six… Well, I suggest you make it work, because we're coming in at six and if a table isn't waiting we're going to break shit. *(Hangs up)* And that is how you book a table! *(To* TOM*)* By the way I'm Larry.

TOM: Tom.

(TOM *goes for a handshake, which* LARRY *snubs, instead plopping his suitcase onto his bed, the left one.)*

LARRY: At least you've got a good sounding name. Piercing without being overly jarring. Some of the best people I've known were named Tom. Larry on the other hand, is an awful fucking name.

TOM: Is it?

LARRY: Abso-fuckin-lutely. But I use the awfulness to my advantage. Whenever I go into a meeting and introduce myself people instantly take me for some used car salesman. Which I am not, but I play the part because it relaxes them. And by the time anyone realizes I've worked them over, the contract is signed and I'm sitting on a beach sipping margaritas in a country with palm trees whose name ends in a vowel.

BARB: Do you want to go over strategy at the table or at the table?

LARRY: How about we do it at the table?

(BARB *gets up with her briefcase and goes to the table. Over the course of the next section she takes things out of her briefcase, setting up a makeshift strategy meeting.*)

TOM: Larry was my uncle's name.

LARRY: Was?

TOM: He passed away a short while ago.

BARB: Sorry.

TOM: It's fine. But thank you.

LARRY: How did he go?

TOM: Cancer.

LARRY: The big C. *(Beat)* You know they say we all get some type of cancer at least five times in our life but our bodies fight it off?

BARB: Sounds like bullshit to me.

LARRY: For your information I read that in a medical journal.

BARB: Why were you reading a medical journal?

LARRY: It was in the office bathroom. *(Beat)* How old are you Tom?

TOM: Thirty-four.

LARRY: That means you've fought off cancer at least once in your life. Barb, you've probably had cancer two, three times.

BARB: Fuck you I'm not that old.

LARRY: Me? I've probably had it three maybe four times by now.

BARB: I'm sorry can we talk about something that's not depressing?

LARRY: It's a sobering concept. All of us spending our lives wrestling with death.

BARB: Death is a fact of life I don't want to think about at three p.m. on a Wednesday.

TOM: *(To* LARRY*)* But if the whole theory is true, you must have good genetics.

LARRY: That I do Tom. Healthy as a motherfucking horse. Hit me.

TOM: Excuse me?

LARRY: In the stomach. And don't go easy. Let me have it.

TOM: Why?

LARRY: To show you how hard my abs are.

TOM: I'll just take your word for it.

LARRY: Come on. You're not going to hurt me.

TOM: I don't think it's appropriate.

LARRY: Why?

TOM: Because we're co-workers.

LARRY: That's such a cop out. I mean tell me you're afraid or that you've never been in a fight, but don't hide behind the whole "corporate thing". Look at where we are. The rules of formal business etiquette do not apply. Barb, when you first came up here what was the first thing you learned?

BARB: That the rules of formal business etiquette do not apply.

TOM: All the same I'm not going to punch you.

LARRY: Well if you change your mind you know where to find me.

BARB: How was your flight?

LARRY: Bumpy as shit and I sat next to a guy who wouldn't shut up. I mean what is it about people on airplanes who feel they have free license to turn to the person next to them and talk their goddamn ear off?

BARB: Why didn't you tell the guy you weren't interested in talking?

LARRY: I would have. But he was twice my size and looked like a killer.

TOM: I think conversation on airplanes is interesting.

LARRY: Sorry?

TOM: I said I think conversation on airplanes is interesting.

LARRY: And how's that.

TOM: I find you can learn a great deal about people by paying attention to what they talk about. Like on the way here I sat next to a woman who talked about different types of traffic across the country. She had this gaze in her eyes. Turned out she was scared of flying and talking about traffic was her coping mechanism.

LARRY: Well. What an odd yet delightfully-told anecdote.

BARB: *(To* LARRY*)* You bring the updated survey report?

LARRY: In my bag top pocket on the left.

*(*BARB *goes to* LARRY*'s bag, opens the tops pocket, takes out a bound report, goes back to the couch and begins to read.)*

LARRY: So new guy. Tell me about yourself.

TOM: What would you like to know?

LARRY: Everything. But lets start with how long you been in with the company.

TOM: Nine months.

LARRY: Bullshit. They don't send newbies up here anymore.

BARB: That's what I said.

LARRY: Means one of two things: either you're full of shit or your dad is on the board.

TOM: My dad is not on the board.

LARRY: Okay then you're full shit.

TOM: All I know is I was sent to help with the numbers: system analytics, speculation / models-—

LARRY: How / long have you been in energy?

TOM: Eight years.

LARRY: And where'd you work before joining Smith?

TOM: Exxon.

LARRY: You get fired?

TOM: No actually I left.

LARRY: Why?

TOM: Because my job there was behind a desk and I wanted to get experience out in the field.

LARRY: So you left the world's fifth largest producer of oil and joined a company with less than five percent U S market share?

TOM: Something like that, yes.

LARRY: ...I see that you're wearing a wedding band.

TOM: Married last year.

LARRY: Kids?

TOM: Expecting our first in July.

LARRY: Tom, do you want to be successful at leasing?

TOM: Of course.

LARRY: Then do your wife a favor and leave her now. I've been doing this job nearly three decades. Guess how many days I travel per year.

TOM: Fifty.

LARRY: Fifty? Jesus Christ he is new. Two hundred days and nights. Living in moldy trailers and bed-bug infested motels. Now granted I'm not exactly the authority on functional relationships, but this much I know—a wife, especially one carrying child, will quickly gain a piercing resentment if they are put in the back seat to their spouse's vocation. And to be successful at this vocation you must always put your wife in the back seat. If you're not comfortable with that, I suggest you crawl back to Exxon and get back your desk job.

TOM: If you'll excuse me I'm going to use the rest room. *(He exits to the bathroom and closes the door.)*

BARB: You're laying it on a little thick, don't you think?

LARRY: How so?

BARB: When the hell have you ever stayed in a bed bug infested motel?

LARRY: All the time. Plenty of times.

BARB: One time.

LARRY: The point is that we're on the threshold of landing the biggest deal of our lives and now here's this kid. I mean that story with the plane. What in the fuck was that about?

BARB: I think you're just making him nervous.

LARRY: What do you make of him so far?

BARB: I think he seems nice.

LARRY: Neatly folded laundry is nice. What do you know about him?

BARB: Besides what he's told you? He's originally from Denver. The way he talks about it I'm guessing he likes to ski.

LARRY: You trust him?

BARB: You know that I don't trust anyone.

LARRY: Neither do I. But does he strike you as capable?

BARB: I think he has ambition.

LARRY: Most young guns do. I know I did. Difference here is this kid happened to stumble into a sure thing.

BARB: Maybe.

LARRY: There's no maybe about it. Jim came to us. That means he's ready. And come tomorrow we're gonna be swimming in champagne and that fancy Caviar from New York that you love.

BARB: Petrossian.

LARRY: Exactly. You're going to have more of that shit than you know what to do with.

BARB: *(Exhales)* Yeah…

LARRY: What's with you Barb?

BARB: What do you mean?

LARRY: You don't have your usual spark.

BARB: My usual spark?

LARRY: It's like you've got a storm cloud hanging over your head. You having boyfriend problems?

BARB: I haven't had a boyfriend in years.

LARRY: Well that's a problem.

BARB: Not really.

LARRY: Okay so then what? Something happening in the Chicago office? Cause if those fuckers are jerking you around I'll personally come down there and break asses.

BARB: It's about the potential sale of Smith Oil.

LARRY: Oh fuck—that shit?

BARB: I heard that there's a good chance it's happening.

LARRY: Barb, I'm telling you it's not. Think about it. Who would be stupid enough to buy Smith? We're small.

BARB: Not that small.

LARRY: Look, if for some ungodly reason Smith Oil is being bought, which it isn't, by the time a sale gets approved by the board and goes through all the legal whatever, we'll be long fucking gone. Floating to Earth on our golden parachutes.

BARB: If we get this lease.

LARRY: We're going to get this lease.

BARB: How do you know?

LARRY: Because this is a defining moment, and in defining moments you kick asses and I take names. Barb, in the past ten years, have I ever let you down? And I'm not talking about doing embarrassing shit at bars. I'm talking about falling short during battle. When we go toe to toe with these fuckers, have I ever not delivered?

BARB: No.

LARRY: Then relax and smile. Smile!

(BARB *shows a smile and gives* LARRY *the finger.*)

LARRY: Okay! There she is. Now guess what I brought with me?

BARB: What?

LARRY: Only your favorite thing in the world.

BARB: You brought Krispy Kreme donuts?

(LARRY *goes to his bag. We hear the toilet flush and the sink turn on.*)

LARRY: Okay I brought your second favorite thing. *(He pulls out a bottle of Johnny Walker Blue Label.)*

BARB: You brought the Blue Label.

LARRY: The only way to celebrate a done deal.

(TOM *re-enters.*)

LARRY: There he is. For a moment I thought you climbed out the bathroom window.

TOM: *(A moment, then getting it.)* Oh. Nope. Can't get rid of me that easy. Also for the record I couldn't hear most of what you said while I was in there.

LARRY: What do you mean? You were listening in on us?

TOM: No, it's just the door is thin and—

LARRY: Alright shut up I don't care. So Barb, what are you thinking for tonight? Tickle Tickle, Shock and Awe or Total Fucking Armageddon?

BARB: Definitely Tickle Tickle.

LARRY: Really?

BARB: Why what do you think?

LARRY: Total fucking Armageddon.

BARB: Bold choice.

LARRY: Well I think we're clearly at that point.

TOM: I'm sorry, what exactly are we talking about?

LARRY: The approach to tonight's dinner!

BARB: Tom think of a business dinner like a symphony. For it to be harmonious you gotta nail the tone.

TOM: Great. So who are the people we're meeting with?

LARRY: I'm sorry?

TOM: Who are the people we're—

LARRY: No I heard you. What I was asking was- do you not understand what's going on here?

TOM: I was told that you'd fill me in on the specifics when I arrived.

LARRY: Excuse me but my job is to do my job, not explain your job to you! I mean shit, next you're gonna tell me this is your first time to North Dakota.

(TOM *says nothing.*)

LARRY: *(To* BARB*)* Holy shit please tell me this isn't his first time to North Dakota.

BARB: Tom? Can you go in the bathroom again? Larry and I need to talk.

TOM: I'd prefer to step outside. The bathroom is a bit claustrophobic and smells funny. *(He walks to the door, forgetting his coat.)*

LARRY: Don't forget your coat.

(TOM *goes to his cot to get his coat,* LARRY *watching him the whole time. As he passes* BARB—*)*

TOM: Let me know when you want me to come back—

(BARB *waves him outside.* TOM *puts on his coat and exits.)*

LARRY: He's never been here before?? Is this some kind of sick fucking joke?!

BARB: Larry it's going to be fine.

LARRY: You're goddamn right it is. Because tonight we're leaving him here. I mean no way are we walking into this dinner with someone who has no idea how this place works.

BARB: Look, corporate wouldn't have sent him if they didn't think he could help.

LARRY: Why are you going to bat for him?

BARB: I'm not. I just think we're facing six people tonight and we need all the firepower we can get. Not to mention what if a question arises about numbers that we don't know the answer to. What are we going to say? "Sorry, we left the numbers guy back in the trailer?" Come on, you know I'm right.

LARRY: ...If it was anyone else asking.

BARB: Thank you.

LARRY: I'm serious, Barb. Not even the Pope or Sinatra. Not even Elvis.

BARB: I said thank you.

LARRY: Don't go thanking me too fast. The kid's not in yet. We still gotta vet him.

(BARB *opens the front door and motions to* TOM, *who re-enters.*)

LARRY: Tom do you want to be apart of what we're doing here?

TOM: Of course.

LARRY: Then stop talking and listen, because what I am about to explain you will need to understand perfectly. Because if you don't it will jeopardize everything Barb and I have been working for, and I will strip butt-naked and impale myself on a rusty pole in the town fucking square before I let that happen. So shut the fuck up and sit down.

(TOM *sits.*)

LARRY: Tonight we are going to dinner with a very important gentleman. His name is Indian Jim.

TOM: Why is he named that?

BARB: Because he is Native American and his name is Jim.

TOM: Do people call him Indian Jim to his face?

LARRY: Of course not! It's highly offensive. *(Beat)* Now
I don't know what you know about Williston, but ten
years ago this was a sleepy cow town with a shit ton of
oil, then the '08 frenzy came and the town got over run
with prospectors—

BARB: Hence why we now stay in a man camp two
miles out of town like we're refugees.

LARRY: Exactly. Now—to most landmen Williston is
old news— Past its peak. Picked over. But this is not
true. Cause while most landowners holding mineral
rights have let oil companies onto their land, there is
one man who has not.

BARB: Indian Jim.

LARRY: Reason being Indian Jim doesn't like the oil
industry. He fucking hates the oil industry. And any
time someone has had the balls to approach Jim for a
lease, he's either shot at them or tried to run them over.
This means everyone has long since given up on Indian
Jim and his land.

BARB: Everyone but us.

LARRY: For the past six years we've been keeping our
presence known: sending Jim cards, leaving Jim voice
mails— Every year I even mail him a box of cigars on
a day which may or may not be his birthday. Now we
don't do this because we enjoy wasting our time—

BARB: We do it because we see the effort as a long term
investment.

LARRY: —So we've waited. *(Beat)* Then last month I'm
at my desk and what do you suppose happens?

TOM: You got a call from Jim?

LARRY: Exactly! So I get ready to answer, but I let
it ring a bit. I mean I don't want this fuck thinking

I'm eager. Finally I pick it up, put the receiver to my mouth… And I don't say a fucking word.

TOM: Why not?

LARRY: I wanted to see what he'd do. I mean here's Jim who's struck the fear of God in every landman he's ever met. Now here's me, a guy who's been hounding his ass for six years straight. And when he finally calls me back, not only do I let the phone ring a few times, but upon answering I don't say a goddamn word? What a mind fuck.

TOM: So what happened?

LARRY: I waited until it felt like the phone was going to explode from tension and I said "Yeah?". Mega pause. He finally says, "Larry. This is Jim." You know what I said? "Jim who?" HA! Larry, one. Jim, zero. BAM! At any rate, once we got past the introductory bullshit he expressed the desire to meet and discuss a lease, and here we are. *(To BARB)* Really the whole thing was the truest example of a signpost that I've ever had the pleasure of encountering.

TOM: What's a signpost?

BARB: It's a theory Larry has about normal everyday occurrences.

LARRY: *(To BARB.)* Signposts are not normal everyday occurrences. They are external beacons, alerts. *(To TOM)* They tell us when to act, when to wait. They warn of trouble ahead. Aside from God himself, signposts are the most divine thing in the world!

TOM: But how is Jim calling you a sign post? Seems pretty straightforward.

LARRY: It is straightforward, Tom. And that's the thing about sign posts. Some are nuanced, and some hit you over the head. *(Beat)* Now you're probably asking yourself "Why does one man matter so much?"

BARB: Because we believe Jim's land holds the last big reserve of oil in the entire region.

TOM: And what makes you think that?

LARRY: Tom where are we?

TOM: North Dakota.

LARRY: This kid...

BARB: He meant geologically, Tom. What is underneath our feet?

TOM: The Williston Basin.

LARRY: Exactly. This basin traps all sorts of shit, but mostly water and oil which are found in same locations at different depths. Now the largest aquifer on the entire northern plains runs directly under Jim's land. So knowing this, we have deduced that underneath that water is a shit ton of oil.

BARB: Also we lease the land around Jim's property, and all of that land has provided us our most productive wells.

TOM: Does Jim know any of this?

LARRY: At some point someone might have given him a rough estimate.
But he didn't hear shit from us. And our shit is the shit that matters. Meaning we have the upper hand in the negotiations.

TOM: So how do we negotiate?

BARB: As I'm sure you know most leases are negotiated via a monthly rate and / or a royalty cut percentage. But what we do up here is come in with a cash advance offer.

LARRY: To these people cash up front is a sign of respect. And respect is the key to the whole damn thing.

TOM: So how much are we offering Jim?

BARB: Based on projections we estimate there's 50 million worth of oil under Jim's land. So we'll offer four.

TOM: Four million?

LARRY: Okay no way we're paying four.

BARB: I'm saying that's our ceiling.

LARRY: Mark my words we're gonna hook his ass at three.

TOM: I'm sorry, that amount seems really low to me.

LARRY: Not when you build in all of our expenses. Fixed costs, state permits, federal permits, repair and restore. Not to mention the tribute to the council.

TOM: What tribute?

BARB: The majority of areas we develop here are under the jurisdiction of tribal nations. So every time we acquire a lease we pay a tribute to the council.

TOM: For how much?

LARRY: Fifty-thousand per well.

BARB: It's what they've deemed equitable for past transgressions we've inflicted upon their nation—

LARRY: Yada yada ya. The point is we low ball the fuckers cause before we even touch the ground we're hemorrhaging money.

TOM: But why are we so intent on dealing with Jim? If we lease the land around him can't we just side drill under his property?

LARRY: Tom, if we could side drill we wouldn't be having this conversation because we'd of already side drilled.

BARB: We've tried, but the soil surrounding his tract is incredibly rocky and it chewed up our drills.

LARRY: It's like an impenetrable fortress out there. Fourteen thousand acres of gorgeous nothingness.

TOM: So why is Jim interested in doing this now?

LARRY: That we don't know.

BARB: Maybe he's gone broke. Or he's dying and trying to get his kids some money.

LARRY: The point is that tonight's dinner is critical to the deal going through, so we are going total fucking Armageddon. That means if at dinner Jim asks you to sing, you don't stop til your voice gives out. If he asks you to stand on the table and jump, you get your ass up there and leap for heaven. We will do anything short of murdering someone and even that is up for debate. Is that clear?

TOM: Completely.

BARB: Great. Now can we please get started?

LARRY: Hold on. Guppy boy isn't out of the woods just yet. *(To* TOM*)* Have you ever been in a fight?

TOM: What?

LARRY: And I'm not talking about an argument or shoving match. I'm talking about a fist-throwing cops-called fight.

TOM: Why does it matter?

LARRY: Because I said it does.

BARB: Larry—

LARRY: Barb I gotta know who I'm sticking my neck out for.
Otherwise when he's getting stomped out by a Hell's Angel high on bath salts I might just keep eating my ribs. *(To* TOM*)* And yes that is something that has

happened before. Now have you or have you not been
in a fight?

TOM: Yes. Though it was a long time ago.

LARRY: Spill it.

TOM: It's kind of an embarrassing story.

LARRY: Even better.

(Beat)

TOM: When I was little I used to take the bus to school.
I was pretty scrawny and so these older kids would
pick on me.

LARRY: How much older?

TOM: I was eight they were twelve. They'd throw stuff
at me and call me names. I usually ignored it or played
along, but one day the ring leader thought it would be
funny to put a big wad of gum in my hair. Everyone
on the bus started laughing. I got really angry. I played
hockey and so I had my skates in my backpack. I
reached in, took out my skate guard, which is like a
little plastic club—

LARRY: I'm from Minnesota I know what a fuckin'
skate guard is.

TOM: Anyway I just went nuts, hitting him in the head
as hard as I could, over and over until blood started
gushing from his face. The bus stopped, the kid passed
out. It was horrible. Later that day I was sitting in
class, completely freaked out about the whole thing,
when the principle walks into my class room and asks
me to come with her. I'm thinking that this is it. That
she's taking me to her office and I'm being expelled
or worse. She leads me to the infirmary and there's
the kid, laying in a bed nearly unconscious, his head
completely bandaged. The principle turns to me and
says "You could have made him go blind." Then she

tells me to go back to class. When I got home I walked through the front door there was mom. She looked at me and asked how my day was. *(With an odd tone of gratification)* The school hadn't called. They never did. *(A new tone of seriousness)* And those kids on the bus never messed with me again.

(A beat)

LARRY: Tom, do you want to come to tonight's dinner?

TOM: Of course.

LARRY: Don't you dare "of course" me. Tonight will be the most important night of your professional life and you've got to yearn to be there with every ounce of your being.

TOM: I do.

LARRY: Then stop being a polite pussy, and start acting like that little kid who decided he was done being fucked with. Do you understand?

TOM: *(A slight intensity)* Perfectly.

(A tense moment between LARRY *and* TOM*)*

BARB: Are you two done measuring dicks now? Because we've got a ton to go over.

(Beat. LARRY *goes to the table, picks up the updated survey report, looks at it in his hand a moment, then hands it back to* BARB.*)*

LARRY: Okay.

BARB: Great.

(Lights fade.)

Scene 2

(That evening at Holidays. BARB, LARRY and TOM either sit or stand together facing the audience. Lighting should isolate them each, and suggest what we are seeing is how each of them are behaving during the dinner. Their "personas". Music should play over this scene that suggests the grinding gears of machinery and metallic moving parts of business. We can hear the sound of everyone's voice but can't quite make out what they are saying. At first they all behave similar, having 'get to know you' chit chats, each with a separate person we do not see. There's bits of laughter from a jokes told be the unseen people peppered in. LARRY begins inquiring about something. BARB is being tough yet seems to be slightly flirty. This is her "I'm sweet but don't fuck with me" approach. TOM begins to loosen up, getting a little intoxicated. LARRY hears something that visibly affects him, but then he forces a smile and keeps talking. TOM is getting more loose and is maybe being told a dirty joke that catches him off guard. He laughs hard, drinking the experience up. LARRY disengages from his conversation and looks at TOM, who is now fully enjoying himself and laughing and talking enthusiastically. BARB notices LARRY and begins to watch him. TOM continues to laugh.)

(Lights fade and the music continues to through the darkness until light rises quickly on the next scene.)

Scene 3

(Later that night)

(BARB, having just entered the trailer, stands inside the door, taking off her coat seemingly mentally preoccupied.)

(TOM is walking to his cot with his coat slung over his shoulder. He seems a bit drunk but not super intoxicated.)

TOM: I thought tonight was really something!

I mean once you peel back the layers, this town is really interesting. *(Beat)* Take that restaurant. Doc Holiday's. From the outside it looks like nothing more than a rusty shed that's half falling apart. But then you go in, and you look around, and wow. Simple yet complex. Elegant yet unpretentious. Barb, if there's one thing in this world that I love, it's when things lack pretension. *(Beat)* But hands down best part of the night?

BARB: The giant moose head over the fireplace.

TOM: How did you know?

BARB: Because you mentioned it three times on the drive home.

TOM: Sorry. I think I'm a little drunk.

BARB: I noticed.

TOM: I didn't want to get drunk. When I'm on business dinners I always limit myself to two drinks. But I was sitting next to Jim's cousin and he kept buying me shots of tequila.

BARB: And vodka. And Rum.

TOM: I forgot about the rum.

BARB: I usually do too.

TOM: I hope I didn't make a fool of myself tonight.

BARB: No. You did great. Most people who consume as much liquor as you did would be face down in a ditch.

TOM: Can I tell you a secret? *(Whisper talk)*I only drank half of every shot. And before Jim's cousin knew the difference I poured the rest in my water glass.

BARB: I saw you doing that.

TOM: You did?

BARB: Not much gets by me. But you definitely had Jim's cousin fooled.

TOM: How do you think dinner went?

BARB: I thought the food was fine.

TOM: I was asking about the meeting.

(LARRY *enters. He looks tired.*)

LARRY: I need a drink.

TOM: Hey Larry. Where you been?

LARRY: I've been sitting outside in the car.

TOM: Why?

LARRY: I needed to think.

TOM: You enjoy dinner?

LARRY: Sure Tom. Dinner was just dandy.

TOM: Yeah, I thought so too.

LARRY: Of course you do. You're shit canned drunk.

TOM: I'm not that drunk.

LARRY: Maybe not yet. But after one of these you will be.

(LARRY *cracks the Johnnie Walker and pours two glasses, one regular, and one to the top of the glass. He holds the tall one out for* TOM, *staring him down.* TOM *takes it.* BARB, *holds out her empty coffee cup to* LARRY, *who looks at her then pours scotch into it.*)

LARRY: In the words of my father, here's to drowning our confusion and sorrows. Down the hatch.

(BARB *takes a sip.* LARRY *downs his whiskey.* TOM *doesn't drink his.* LARRY *notices.*)

LARRY: What's the matter Tom? You don't like Scotch?

TOM: No I do. I just don't understand why we're standing around like it's a funeral. I thought tonight went great.

LARRY: You know, maybe you are that drunk. Because if you weren't, you'd know that tonight's dinner was a fucking train wreck.

TOM: I don't see how you can say that.

LARRY: Jim wasn't there! And the whole point of tonight was to go to dinner with JIM and convince JIM that leasing us the land was in his best interests.

TOM: His family was there.

LARRY: You bet they were. All his brothers and sisters. Even his grand kids.

BARB: Luckily at Holidays kids eat for free.

TOM: It's possible they were his scouts.

LARRY: The grand kids?

TOM: Everyone who was there.

BARB: What do you mean?

TOM: Maybe this is how Jim operates. He calls up companies and tells them he wants to meet. But instead of going himself he sends his family.

BARB: And he would do that why?

TOM: All I'm saying is when I was in college I was on the crew team, and whenever a new recruit came in, coach would tell him to go to the boathouse at seven am on Saturday and wait until he arrived. The recruit would show up but coach wouldn't be there. Nine o clock that night, coach would show up, and if the kid was still there, he'd give him a shot.

LARRY: So what you're saying is, we're the recruit and Jim is the coach?

TOM: It was just an example. But yes.

BARB: Crazy. But interesting.

LARRY: No Barb, it's not interesting. We're talking about a business transaction not some rowing tryout. With these people it's always about the money and the reason Jim didn't come tonight is because someone else got to him first.

BARB: How do you know?

LARRY: Because I just called him to confirm tomorrow's meeting.

BARB: What did he say?

LARRY: Nothing. It went to voice mail.

BARB: You try calling him back?

LARRY: Three times. Same thing each time.

TOM: Maybe he was on the phone.

LARRY: It's eleven Tom, so I highly doubt it.

BARB: I don't get this at all.

LARRY: Me neither. But I'm too fucking tired. *(Beat)* Either way it's finished.

TOM: Respectfully, I think you're giving up on this too easily.

LARRY: Excuse me?

TOM: You said it yourself, the guy thinks oil companies are scum. But he's seen what's been happening all around town with everything getting built up and developed. He's fought the good fight, but now he figures it's just a matter of time before he gets bought up too. But he wants to make sure he's dealing with someone who will treat him with respect, so he sent his family to dinner to see how we would treat them. Jim is looking for a friend.

(LARRY begins to laugh to himself. He goes and pours himself another drink.)

LARRY: Tom, I wasn't sure about you when you first arrived. But now I know without a doubt that you are a fucking Boy Scout.

TOM: And how's that, Larry?

BARB: Okay it's been a long day and we're all on edge.

LARRY: *(A bit sharp)* Excuse me Barb, but Tom and I are talking. If you don't mind.

BARB: *(With an edge)* No problem. *(She exits to the bathroom with her drink, closing the door behind her.)*

LARRY: Now where were we? That's right. You wanted to know what makes you a Boy Scout. You really want to know?

TOM: I do.

LARRY: Okay. You're a Boy Scout because reality is staring you right in the fucking eyes and you're too damn naive to see it.

TOM: And what reality is that?

LARRY: Jim's grandfather was in the trail of fucking tears. To him we are the pale faced invaders, the destroyers of purity, the devil fucking incarnate! And you think this great plains-roaming stick-wielding fuck wants to be friends with us?!

TOM: Has it occurred to you that maybe Jim didn't come to dinner because of your reputation?

LARRY: And what is my reputation?

TOM: That you're known for saying offensive things.

LARRY: So you're saying that Jim didn't come to tonight's dinner specifically because I say offensive things.

TOM: Tonight his cousin mentioned that you show a lack of respect.

LARRY: Jesus Christ of course he told you that! This is warfare, Tom! They are trying to divide us. But you wouldn't know that because you're too busy thinking you've got this whole place figured out, which is an insult to those of us who actually do!!

TOM: Larry you don't know me.

LARRY: Yes I do. Because I know your generation. All talk all the time. I watched you at dinner and you were just having a ball. Spouting off this fact and that fact. A real fucking expert. Tell me something- why do you think you know everything about everything? Is it that you think you're intellectually superior? Cause you're not. Here's a pro tip—you learn shit by earning shit. And you haven't earned a fucking thing.

TOM: And you have?

LARRY: You're god damn right. I grew up in a family of people who didn't just work, they labored. The only tools my dad had were these *(holds up his hands.)* He spent his life in a mill so he could provide for his family and in the end he barely had enough money to buy a coffin!! I spent the first five years of my career doing every shit bucket task with a smile tattooed on my face—not because I enjoyed the punishment, but because I was earning my spot here now. How'd you get here? Spend a couple hundred grand of your daddy's money to get a degree that gave some H R vampire a hard on?

TOM: Larry if I wanted to hear another story about how the older generation is wiser and young people don't know shit I'd visit my grandparents in Nebraska.

LARRY: You little motherfucker.

(LARRY advances on TOM. BARB comes out of the bathroom.)

BARB: Okay that's enough.

LARRY: I look at you and I see someone who's never had to fight for what's theirs.

BARB: I said that's enough.

LARRY: Everything you have has just been given to you and it makes me want to fucking puke!

BARB: STOP IT, STOP IT!! …Just stop it!

TOM: I think it's best if I step out a moment. Excuse me. *(He puts on a coat and leaves through the front door.)*

BARB: What in the fuck was that?

LARRY: That was me telling it like it is. I mean Jesus! I feel like I'm the only one who has the guts to tell the truth anymore.

BARB: And what category does calling Jim a "great-plains roaming, stick-wielding fuck" fall under?

LARRY: That was perhaps a tad much.

BARB: You think?

LARRY: Okay I totally went thermal.

BARB: I've never seen you lose it like that before.

LARRY: Well I've never felt like this. Fuck, Barb. I could taste it. It was right there. And then, it wasn't.

BARB: Larry.

LARRY: I think I'll go out for a while.

BARB: You shouldn't drive.

LARRY: Excuse me but you're not my keeper.

(Beat. LARRY exits. BARB goes to the window and looks out at him. We hear his car turn on and see light from the headlights drive off. BARB walks around the space, visibly upset about everything that just happened. After a moment TOM enters through the front door.)

TOM: I waited to come back in until he was gone.

BARB: What makes you think you can talk to him like that?

TOM: I got upset.

BARB: Well next time you want to get into it with someone thirty years your senior, swallow your pride and shut up!!

TOM: You're right. I escalated things. I apologize.

(A moment, then BARB *sits on her bed.)*

TOM: For the record, some of the stuff he said was true. I've definitely worked hard to get where I am, but some H R person did see my degree and get a hard on.

BARB: Were you really on the crew team?

TOM: Placed third at nationals two years in a row. Pardon the pun.

BARB: Where'd you go?

TOM: I'd rather not say.

BARB: What? Did you go to Yale or something?

*(*TOM *says nothing.)*

BARB: Hold on you went to Yale?

TOM: They offered me a scholarship and I couldn't pass it up.

BARB: Jesus.

TOM: I know it's snooty but the education I got was great.

BARB: What I meant is that I can relate.

TOM: What? Did you go to Yale too?

BARB: Hell no. *(Beat)* I went to Princeton.

TOM: No shit?

BARB: My father was a legacy.

(Beat)

TOM: I'm going to have another. You want one?

BARB: Sure.

(TOM *pours them both another drink. He sits on the other bed.*)

TOM: Why is a person like you working in this field?

BARB: What? You think a woman can't work in oil?

TOM: No they certainly can. But what leads a graduate of Princeton University to become a leasing rep?

BARB: An affinity for masochism. That and when I graduated I was recruited by JP Morgan and Smith Oil and Smith offered me twice the salary. What about you?

TOM: I was recruited by Exxon and Google. *(Beat)* So what got you up here?

BARB: It's where my career took me.

TOM: Okay. But there has to be a story involved.

BARB: Why?

TOM: Because women don't get sent to North Dakota to conduct this type of business like ever. So either you were sent here because you are like the most ruthless person ever or you were sent here to fail. Which you haven't. Which potentially circles things back to the above said conclusion that you're ruthless.

BARB: You know if this oil thing doesn't work out for you you'd make a great T V detective.

TOM: I'm just curious about your story.

BARB: Why?

TOM: I'd like us to get to know each other better.

BARB: *(Sarcastic.)* Tom? I'm flattered. But I'm a decade older and you're married.

TOM: No! That's not what I - shit, that totally came out wrong.

BARB: Relax. I knew what you meant. And yes, for the record, I was in fact sent here to fail.

TOM: Why? Come on. We're having a drink and we gotta talk about something.

BARB: Five years after I joined the Chicago office corporate brought in this grade A tool bag for regional director. Will Gun.

TOM: Wait, that was his real name?

BARB: Couldn't make it up if I tried. He liked to walk around the office pointing his fingers at people pretending he was shooting them.

TOM: I have to say—that's amazingly awesome.

(BARB *and* TOM *share a small laugh but then she gets more serious.*)

BARB: He used to play these "jokes". Taking people's chairs, moving desks, but never doing anything to me. One day we were in the elevator together. I'm standing there thinking about what's for dinner, when I feel this hand slowly run down my back and stop right above my ass. Then he whispered into my ear "I see the way you look at me. Let's go to my place." I politely told him to fuck off. The next morning the way everyone glanced at me I knew something was up. I went to my desk, opened my top drawer, and it was full of tampons soaked red with a note— "That time of the month?" He was standing there with this smirk. "Don't cry," he said. "It's not real blood."

TOM: So what'd you do?

BARB: I closed the drawer and got to work.

TOM: I can't believe you just took it.

BARB: I didn't. I waited for our next conference call with headquarters, and as he was giving quarterly projections I began to ask him every question I knew he didn't know the answer to until he exploded into a tantrum. He got fired that afternoon. The next day I got a call from Old Man Smith. At first I thought he was firing me too, which would have been a mistake cause I would've unleased the lawsuit from hell. But he wasn't. He was calling to tell me I was being re-assigned to North Dakota. And here I am—The Smith Oil Queen of North Dakota.

TOM: But it does seem like you enjoy it here. In a weird sarcastic way.

BARB: At first I hated it. For the obvious reasons. But over the years I've grown used to it. Plus coming here gets me away from my family.

TOM: How so?

BARB: My parents God bless 'em are convinced I'm destroying the Earth. Email chains about global warming, lectures on the evils of fracking during holiday dinners. But when I bring up the fact that they both drive gas guzzling S U Vs, they tell me they voted for Obama both times.

TOM: Sounds like how my parents used to be. Except they never drove S U V's.

BARB: What do you mean used to be?

TOM: My freshman year of high school both my parents died.

BARB: You're kidding.

TOM: No. It was a car accident. Which in retrospect is ironic because they tried to avoid driving like it was the plague.

BARB: Oh my God. I'm sorry.

TOM: Thank you but it's okay. I mean for a long time it wasn't. After it happened I emotionally fell apart and became a mess. But then my uncle took me in. And now here I am, about to have my own family. That's why coming up here was so important for me. This might sound stupid, but I want to create something my child will inherit.

(Beat)

BARB: Tom there's something you should know.

TOM: Don't tell me I've had something on my face this entire time.

BARB: No. Smith Oil is being bought out.

TOM: By whom?

BARB: I just know it's a company based out of Houston meaning it could be anyone. And based upon the amount of flights my regional director has taken between Houston and Chicago the past few weeks I'm guessing it's happening soon. This is something very few people know about.

TOM: You know about it.

BARB: Because it's my job to know things.

TOM: So why are you telling me?

BARB: Because you're young and about to be a father, and because now that this meeting's imploded there's no reason to pretend the sale isn't happening. *(She gets up and pours herself a bit more scotch.)*

TOM: So what will you do?

BARB: I don't know.

TOM: You don't strike me as the not knowing type.

BARB: I'm not. I've always had a plan. I've always been fighting against something or chasing after the next deal. The feeling I used get after landing a deal? Wasn't a drug on Earth that could match it.

TOM: So you don't enjoy this job anymore?

BARB: It's just you do this job long enough and the kill loses it's thrill.

(A moment, then—)

TOM: Okay. So do something new.

BARB: *(Sarcastic.)* Gee, Tom. Do something new. Why didn't I think of that?

TOM: Come on. I'm serious. What if right here right now there was an opportunity to do something new?

BARB: There's not.

TOM: But what if there was?

BARB: But there isn't.

TOM: But what if there was. And it was new and better and could potentially change everything.

BARB: Look it's late and I'm tired, so why don't you just say whatever it is you're trying to say.

TOM: Water.

BARB: Water?

The table phone rings. Barb goes to it and answers.

BARB: Hello? *(Caught off guard.)* Yes, hi. Okay. Hold on. *(She holds the phone out for* TOM *with a puzzled look on her face.)* It's Jim's cousin. He wants to talk to you.

*(*TOM *goes to the phone.* BARB *watches.)*

TOM: Hi. Okay. Great. What time? Alright see you tomorrow at seven sharp. *(He hangs up the phone.)*

BARB: What in the fuck was that?

TOM: Barb. There's something you should know.

*(*BARB *looks at* TOM. *Lights quick fade)*

Scene 4

(The next morning. The sheets on BARB's *bed are messed up from sleep. There is sun light peeking through the blinds. The room is empty.)*

(The sheets on TOM's *cot are distressed but his suitcase is packed.)*

(We hear a car pull up outside the room. After a moment BARB *enters wearing jeans and a coat. She's holding an 8" x ll" envelope.)*

(She goes to the bathroom door, looking inside.)

(She exhales and sits on her bed, looking at the envelope in her hand. After a moment she packs up some of her things, then exits to the bathroom, closing the door behind her.)

(We hear a car pull up outside. After a moment the door opens and LARRY *enters, carrying a box of Go Go donuts. He's in his clothes from the night before and he looks a bit dishevelled.)*

LARRY: Anyone here?! Barb? *(He puts the donuts down and goes to the bathroom and opens the door.)*

*(*LARRY *sees* BARB *and quick slams the door shut.)*

LARRY: Shit! Sorry!

*(*BARB *comes out a tad pissed off.)*

BARB: Are we not knocking anymore?

LARRY: I didn't think anyone was here.

BARB: My car's out front.

LARRY: I know but when I came in no one answered so I figured— Not that it's anything I haven't seen before.

BARB: What does that mean?

LARRY: I'm just saying, over the years I've seen things. You've seen things.

BARB: It's a little early to be talking about 'things'.

LARRY: I'm just saying.

BARB: I was worried sick about you!

LARRY: Why?

BARB: You didn't come back last night and I called your phone like fifteen times and I thought you were in jail or dead.

LARRY: Oh I'm not dead Barb. Not by a long shot. I'm alive! Alive like I've never been!

BARB: Okay are you on coke right now?

LARRY: I've had a lot of coffee.

BARB: You just getting back?

LARRY: What gave it away? The smell or the clothes?

BARB: Both.

LARRY: Did Tom leave?

BARB: No.

LARRY: Good. I don't want him to miss this.

BARB: Miss what?

LARRY: Barb. We're going to salvage this trip!

BARB: Larry hold on—

LARRY: Now just hear me out. I know things last night went about as horrible as they could go, but it's still there for us. We just need to go get it.

BARB: Larry listen you don't—

LARRY: NO BARB YOU LISTEN. *(Beat)* When I drove out of here last night I was so sickened and disheartened, I just wanted to ride off into the sunset. *(Beat)* But then something happened.

BARB: What?

LARRY: I went to a bar.

BARB: That's not exactly a revelation.

LARRY: It's what happened at the bar. *(Beat)* It was the one we used to go to with the one armed bartender who had all the stories about Vietnam.

BARB: Mickey's.

LARRY: Yes. Mickey's. I'm sitting at the bar and the place is pretty dead. I mean it's Wednesday at midnight. And in walks this guy. I don't look up because I'm in a terrible mood and I figure he's probably just another townie or roughneck looking to tie one on. But there's something about this guy. I mean he's got this loud booming voice and sharp laugh and he just won't shut up. I try to ignore him but the more I try the more he bothers me. So finally I pound my fist on the bar and I scream "SHUT THE FUCK UP". *(Beat)* The whole place goes silent. There's no "Fuck you" back, no bum rush, not even a thrown bottle. But there's something about that silence that tells me I've pushed it too far. Then I hear these boots start walking towards me. "Ah ha. Here it comes." And I'm just waiting for it. And those boots stop right next to me. Then nothing. Now I'm getting mad cause I don't know what the hell this guy is waiting for. So I clench my fists and I turn to clobber this guy and that's when I see it. The barrel of 44 Magnum pointed right at me. The guy says "Get up and walk out the door."

BARB: Jesus what did you do?

LARRY: I had a gun pointed at my face. I got up and walked out the door.

BARB: And no one tried to help you?

LARRY: No. *(Beat)* So we're in the parking lot and he asks which car is mine. I show him and we get in. He tells me to drive. We're on a road headed out of town. I ask where we're going but the guy doesn't say anything, just keeps the gun pointed at me. He tells me to stop. We walk out into this field. It's pitch black. I hear the wind blowing through the grass. There's this aroma in the air. Sweet like flowers. The man tells me to get on my knees. I ask if we can be reasonable about this. I hear him pull back the hammer. I consider the possibility of running, but to where? *(Beat)* I get on my knees. And I start to cry. I cry like a baby. It all pours out of me. Then I wait for it. Five seconds. Ten. Still nothing. I ask "Are you going to do it or what?" I don't get a response. I turn around. He's gone. Then I hear this voice in the breeze. "Wake up." Then I woke up. I was in Mickey's. Slumped over the bar.

BARB: So you had a dream.

LARRY: Yes. But it felt so real. I mean I was thinking and conscious. It made me realize something.

BARB: What?

LARRY: All these years I've always considered myself the one in charge. But when I was in the field on my knees staring out into the darkness, I saw that it's never been me. It's been you.

BARB: That's not true.

LARRY: Bullshit. Even the first time we met. You came in the room wearing pumps and a skirt and I said to myself, "Jesus. This chick won't last a day.". But then we got to the meeting for the Kirby Ranch lease and no matter how hard I pressed the guy wouldn't budge. I mean fuck, why would he? The guy was a cattle man sentimental about his herd.Ê

The whole deal was going down in flames until you stepped in. You told him that you understood his hesitation, but that he should think it through. You said, and I'll never forget this, 'why work on your feet all day raising cattle when you can sit on your ass raising gold?' ...BAM! He signed the lease, the biggest Smith had landed, and I knew I'd found a real partner.

Someone who understood the way things worked. Barb the truth is that you're the best fucking landman I've ever met, and you deserve this deal more than anyone. This is the moment from which all our other moments will be measured. This is the moment that will define our very lives.

BARB: Larry I have to tell you something.

LARRY: Look I get it, our backs are against the wall and you're scared.

BARB: No that's not—

LARRY: Barb it's fine. I'm scared too. But this is not the time to give into fear.

BARB: Would you stop?!

LARRY: You stop! We are warriors! We score deals! This is who we are!

BARB: Larry you're ranting!

LARRY: I'm calling it like it is!! And as long as we're here and Jim is out there on his land we've still got a fighting chance. So have a donut, get dressed and put your game face on because we're going to nail that fucker to the wall. *(Beat)* Now if you'll excuse me I need to shower I smell like shit. *(He gets up and exits to bathroom. He turns on the shower. We can faintly hear him singing or humming.)*

(A throaty diesel truck pulls up outside. Then we hear it drive off. After a moment TOM enters in a cowboy hat, jeans and a tucked in long sleeve button up. He has a leather briefcase.)

TOM: Hey.

BARB: Hey.

TOM: I see Larry's back.

BARB: Yep.

TOM: Good. When did he—

BARB: About ten minutes ago.

TOM: Where was he?

BARB: It's a long story.

TOM: There's donuts.

BARB: He brought them.

(TOM *takes a donut. Offers one to* BARB)

BARB: No thanks.

TOM: You bring him up to speed?

BARB: I tried to.

TOM: Not a problem. I'll tell him. *(Beat)* I have to say, that plot of land is so beautiful. After the meeting you really shoulda come along on the tour. Jim's truck had plenty of room.

BARB: It was more important to make sure the documents were in order.

TOM: Where are they?

(BARB *points to the bed.* TOM *goes over and takes a quick look.)*

TOM: God that was some meeting. I mean I've never been greeted at a property line by guys carrying loaded rifles. It was like a wild west movie. Then we all sat at that table and the way Jim was staring at us it felt like he was looking into my soul!

BARB: It's all part of their tactic.

TOM: Looking into souls?

BARB: Making the environment as uncomfortable as possible.

TOM: Well mission accomplished. I've never been so nervous.

BARB: You didn't look it.

TOM: I was thinking about pizza.

BARB: What?

TOM: Something my uncle taught me. When you're in a tense situation concentrate on something you love. Also, you were there. And there's no way I would've survived that meeting without you. You were the key to this whole thing. The first of many deals.

(From the shower LARRY *hums louder for a moment.)*

BARB: How are we going to tell him?

TOM: Larry?

BARB: Yes.

TOM: I've found the best way to handle these types of things is with honesty.

BARB: This is going to kill him.

TOM: I think Larry's tougher than that.

BARB: He came back here intent on going out to Jim's to get the lease.

TOM: Really?

BARB: Yes. This deal was everything to him. And I helped take it away from him.

(The shower turns off.)

TOM: I get that you feel bad. I mean you've been Larry's partner up here for ten years. But you're a professional, Barb. And today you did your job. Besides, what we're doing now is a whole new thing. A bigger and better thing.

*(*LARRY *exits the bathroom wearing his pants and a white undershirt. He and* TOM *take each other in a moment.)*

LARRY: Hi Tom.

TOM: Hi Larry.

LARRY: I see you found the donuts.

TOM: Hope you don't mind that I'm having one.

LARRY: It's what I got em for. *(Beat)* So about last night. The things I said came from a place of frustration.

TOM: I can understand that.

LARRY: No hard feelings. Okay?

TOM: Of course.

LARRY: Good. *(Beat)* I've got to say, that's quite the get up you're wearing. Perfect for the meeting.

TOM: The meeting?

LARRY: I've decided we're gonna to head out to Jim's and get that lease. That's what we came here to do and we're gonna do it.

TOM: Larry—

LARRY: I've been thinking about what you said about how Jim was just testing us. I think you were right. I mean who knows? He might be out there with the lease signed and all we have to do is go out there and get it.

TOM: We got the land.

LARRY: What?

TOM: I said we got the land.

LARRY: The fuck are you talking about?

TOM: That's where I just came back from.

LARRY: I don't understand.

TOM: Let's sit.

LARRY: I'll stand. Now you were saying?

TOM: It's all taken care of.

LARRY: How is that possible?

TOM: Because not more than an hour ago Jim and I struck a deal.

LARRY: Bullshit. There's no way.

BARB: Larry—

LARRY: There's no way in hell you did that.

TOM: Why not?

LARRY: Because it's fucking impossible!

TOM: I have no reason to lie to you.

LARRY: I want to see the paperwork.

TOM: Barb?

(A beat. BARB *holds up the envelope for* LARRY. *She cannot look him in the eyes. He snatches the envelope, reads the papers, then lowers them.)*

LARRY: This isn't for a lease. It's an agreement to purchase.

TOM: I know.

LARRY: And that's a disaster. I mean we don't buy land. We never buy land. The tax implications alone—

TOM: I know it's not ideal. But as it turns out Jim isn't interested in leasing. He wants someone to buy him out. So that's what we're going to do.

LARRY: For ten million fucking dollars!?

TOM: That's right.

LARRY: Who in the hell authorized this?!

TOM: I know you're upset. You're the one who's put in the time where as I'm the one who just came in. But the thing is we're on the same team. And we won.

*(*LARRY *cold clocks* TOM *across the jaw, sending him to the ground.)*

BARB: Larry you're out of line!

LARRY: I'm out of line? Jesus Barb. We only get commissions off of leases, not land sales. That slippery little fuck destroyed our deal!

BARB: We never had a chance.

LARRY: What do you mean?

BARB: I thought we had more time. I thought the sale was happening at the end of the month.

LARRY: What sale?

BARB: Of Smith Oil.

LARRY: Okay. Now you're not making any sense either. Can someone in this trailer please start to make some goddamn sense?!

BARB: Smith Oil was bought out before we came up here.

LARRY: Bullshit we would have heard.

BARB: The board has been keeping it a secret.

LARRY: Why would they do that??

BARB: Because of Jim's land! That's the reason Smith was bought. It's the reason Tom is here.

LARRY: Tom's here because he's the numbers guy.

BARB: Actually he's not.

LARRY: Then who the hell is he? Who are you, Tom?

TOM: I'm Thomas Fletcher. Nephew of the late Larry Fletcher and the new Chief Executive Officer of Fletcher Industries. We now own Smith Oil. And you work for me.

(LARRY *looks around a moment not knowing how to react, after a moment processing what's going on he turns to* TOM.)

LARRY: I knew it. I knew it I knew I knew it. *(He sits on the cot.)* Right from the start I knew there was something off about you.

TOM: I guess there's no fooling you Larry.

LARRY: Tom you couldn't fool me if you tried. Either of us. *(To* BARB*)* Jesus Christ, Barb, the restraint you're showing is unbelievable. How you're not jumping through the ceiling right now beats me.

BARB: He told me last night.

LARRY: What?

BARB: I found out last night.

LARRY: *(Beat)* Were you at the meeting?

BARB: When you walked through the door I tried to tell you what was happening but you were going on and on and—

LARRY: Yes or no were you there?!

BARB: Yes.

*(*LARRY *says nothing.)*

BARB: Larry I know it's shitty, but this is the beginning of something better—

LARRY: You shouldn't have gone without me.

BARB: It was important I be there—

LARRY: We're partners!!! *(Beat)* After everything we've been through…

BARB: I'm sorry.

*(*LARRY *goes to the whiskey, unscrews the top and takes a pull. A beat. Then—)*

LARRY: *(To* TOM*)* I don't understand the point of this.

TOM: What do you mean?

LARRY: Fletcher is huge. You have operations in over thirty states. Why go to the trouble of buying Jim's land? It's a drop in the bucket.

TOM: Ever since I started working for my uncle I'd hear him talk about North Dakota. He always wanted to operate up here but he never pulled the trigger. So I came here to start my legacy by acquiring the last big parcel of undeveloped land that was rumored to be unobtainable.

LARRY: But how does Smith figure in? Why go through this charade? Why not just go to Jim directly??

TOM: I did. I called him a month ago. To say he doesn't like oil companies or outsiders is the understatement of the century. Though I did get him to tell me that he was already beginning negotiations with you.

LARRY: So you bought Smith to get access to Jim.

TOM: Yes.

LARRY: Fuck. To spend that kinda money you must really love oil.

TOM: I do. But the reason Jim sold is because I agreed not to drill for oil.

LARRY: But the entire reason we're here is to drill oil.

TOM: Larry what geographically lies beneath us? And what other resource exists here in abundance?

LARRY: *(Beat)* Water.

TOM: The resources that have given this country wealth are disappearing. And not too far off in the future the most sought after resource won't be oil, it'll be clean drinking water. With the acquisition of this land, Fletcher Industries will become the owner of one of the biggest sources of ground water in the northern plains. Granted with water the profits aren't quite there yet, but overall it's a cleaner operation harvesting a renewable resource. That's how I sold it to Jim, and I never would have thought of this angle had you not told me about the aquifer, so thank you.

LARRY: What was the point of you coming up here pretending to be the new guy?

TOM: There aren't many old schoolers like you two out in the field anymore. So I went undercover to get an unbiased assessment of your abilities.

LARRY: So what's the verdict?

TOM: *(Directed at* BARB*)* I found a new regional director.

(A beat)

LARRY: And there it is.

BARB: Larry listen to me—

LARRY: *(Forceful)* Just stop! *(Then lighter to* TOM*)* So where does that leave me.

TOM: I think you possess a great depth of knowledge.

LARRY: I'm talking about my job.

BARB: I think that's a conversation to have another time.

TOM: It's fine. This is as good a time to talk about it as any. *(Beat)* I'm not making any immediate changes.

LARRY: But?

TOM: But in looking over the books it's my opinion that the Minneapolis office is, redundant.

BARB: What?

TOM: I looked over the figures and they just don't add up.

*(*LARRY *laughs to himself.)*

LARRY: You're right. The Minneapolis office is redundant. That's the way Old Man Smith liked to operate things. By the way, now that I know you're my boss what should I call you?

TOM: You can call me Tom.

LARRY: You don't mind?

TOM: The rules of formal business etiquette do not apply. Now you were saying?

LARRY: There's no denying that we've bumped heads a bit. But the thing about me Tom is I am who I am. I'm a killer. Just like Barb. Just like you.

TOM: You think that I'm a killer?

LARRY: I know you're a killer. And I mean that in the best way. That's why you're here. Why we're all here. Because we're drawn to places like this. It's in our nature to set off into the unknown. To conquer something. To leave our mark. It's what gets us out of bed. The bottle of Johnny Walker? You know why Barb and I crack one of those after every deal we land?

TOM: Because it's an expensive scotch.

LARRY: No! Well, yes, sure that too. But we crack that scotch because it's a symbol of the fruit that blossoms from dedication and commitment. *(Beat)* Now look, I know I'm old school and that some of my viewpoints can be viewed as offensive. But I possess value, Tom. I'm not redundant. And I can be of great use to you.

TOM: How?

LARRY: You need someone handling the day to day who understands this place. Things must be done very carefully and anyone who steps out of line gets squashed. Perfect example, five years ago B P comes up here, leases a huge plot for way too much money, brings in the best of everything. Not two months go by and the North Dakota Department of Health and

Environment shuts them down. Wanna know why?..
Over a bunny.

TOM: A bunny?

LARRY: A little bunny having a little bit of lunch with
his bunny family. They're all out there on B P's land
minding their business when along comes this truck
just barreling though, doesn't see the bunny and
(Claps).

TOM: You're telling me that one of the biggest oil
companies in the world got shut down because they
ran over a bunny.

LARRY: But it wasn't just a bunny, Tom. It was an
endangered long ear snow hare. And running over
endangered animals is the type of thing that really
chaps Phil Gurda's ass.

TOM: Who?

LARRY: He's the D H E rep in Williston and he just
loves to jam people up, especially newbies flush in
money. However Phil and I are pals, and for my
friends I can keep him at bay.

TOM: But if I let you go, you'll turn Phil loose on me?

LARRY: What?

TOM: Isn't that what you just implied?

LARRY: That's not what I was— What I was saying is
that this place is a logistical mine field and you will
need help navigating the landscape. So let me help
you.

TOM: I appreciate the offer but I'm going to decline.

LARRY: Tom you can't decline! This is the entire
fucking playbook!! Look, if it's an issue of money I can
take less.

BARB: Larry.

LARRY: Right now I'm at eighty a year but I can go to seventy. *(A beat)* I don't need dental either. *(A beat)* Okay sixty-five. *(Another terrible beat)* Sixty.

BARB: Tom.

LARRY: *(A bit desperate)* Fifty-eight.

BARB: Tom for fuck sake!

TOM: Larry you're going to get a more than reasonable severance package.

LARRY: I DON'T NEED SEVERANCE I NEED THIS. Tell me what I have to do and I'll do it. I'll dress different. I'll start using email. For fuck's sake I'll even stop swearing.

TOM: Larry, there's a lot of sayings my uncle had that have stuck with me, but there's one in particular that sticks out.
The wise man keeps fighting because he knows he can still win. But the delusional man keeps fighting because he doesn't realize he's already lost. The fact is, never in a million years would I let someone like you represent me ever.

LARRY: You piece of shit.

(LARRY shoves TOM, who retreats.)

BARB: *(Standing in LARRY's way)* Larry don't do something stupid.

LARRY: STAY THE HELL OUT OF THIS. *(He pushes past BARB. To TOM)* I see you from a mile away. You think it's okay to treat me like human garbage? Like I'm some figment of the past to be pitied and thrown away? Well fuck you. *(He slowly advances on TOM.)* You're just a scared little pussy hiding behind his wallet. Isn't that right? I said isn't that right!?!?

(LARRY stands inches from TOM, who stares back at him calmly.)

TOM: Larry I let you hit me before because I thought I deserved it. But you hit me now and there will be consequences.

(After a moment, LARRY disengages. He gets his bag, puts on his coat, walks to the door and opens it. Larry looks at both of them, broken, and exits, leaving the door open. We hear a car start and then drive off. A moment, then TOM goes to the door and closes it. He turns back to BARB who's looking at him.)

BARB: You didn't tell me about Minneapolis.

TOM: I'm sorry. I know you two were close and that is not how I wanted that to happen. *(A beat, then Tom begins to get his things together. BARB just watches him.)* Our flight to Houston leaves in an hour so we should think about getting to the airport. Oh and my assistant upgraded you to first class. *(TOM looks up and sees BARB staring at him.)* Look, I understand if you're upset, but don't let personal feelings cloud your professional judgement.

BARB: You want professional Judgement?? What you just did to that man was a disgrace.

TOM: What was I supposed to do? Give Larry a job I didn't want him to have?

BARB: You were supposed to treat him with dignity because that's something he's earned.

TOM: And how has Larry earned dignity? By referring to Jim as a stick wielding fuck?

BARB: Okay Tom, you can drop the "good guy in the white hat" routine cause nobody's buying it anymore.

TOM: What does that mean?

BARB: From the moment you walked in this trailer everything that's come out of your mouth has either been bullshit or lies.

TOM: That's not true.

BARB: Really? So you'd categorize your actions the past twenty-four hours as honest?

TOM: Barb I don't know what-

BARB: You just referred to water rights as an "angle".

TOM: So?

BARB: So the truth is when the deal's finalized we're gonna fuck Jim over.

TOM: No.

BARB: Sure we are. And last night you fed me the spiel about wanting to do things in a new and better way so that I'd be effective at selling your lie.

TOM: Barb water can be a viable option and we're going to do everything we can to—

BARB: Stop lying and tell the truth!!

TOM: Apologize. Don't ask.

(Beat)

BARB: What the fuck does that mean?

TOM: It means that when we do begin to drill for oil, we extend our sincerest apologies to Jim.

BARB: But why apologize, Tom? The land will be yours and you can do whatever you want with it. Rezone, build a refinery. After the oil's gone convert the whole place into a landfill. Better yet a toxic waste dump. Biohazards, radiated material. Excellent money in that.

TOM: Barb the way you're confronting me right now is very hurtful.

BARB: Well fuck you very much. Because I see you for exactly what you are.

TOM: And what's that?

BARB: You're the next generation of the same old shit. And you came here to get yours no matter the cost.

TOM: What I am is a businessman trying to grow a company that I will one day pass to my son. Which I might add is something that you and Larry used to ritualize with a whiskey bottle. Barb, you can act as sanctimonious as you want, but everything I'm doing now you've done longer.

BARB: Jesus Christ of course I have!! You know, when my family gangs up on me about what I do, I just get so pissed off- because I know that what they're saying is true. Over the years I've done lots of shit I'm not proud of, but using water as bait to fuck over a dying old man? That's the limit for me. That's a line I'm not willing to cross.

TOM: Barb you can talk about limits and lines all you want, but the work we do is necessary and it has a cost. And we're not fucking anyone over. If Jim is stupid enough to sign a contract without reading the fine print, then that's on him.

BARB: God, you don't even have a clue what I'm talking about, do you? And you're so blinded by your own ambition that you don't see how wide open you've left yourself.

TOM: What are you talking about?

BARB: I'm talking about respect, Tom. At that meeting you gave Jim your word that you'd protect that land. Now that sort of thing clearly doesn't matter to you, but to Jim it's everything. And if you put so much as a single oil well out on that tract, your actions will be viewed as extremely disrespectful.

TOM: What people think doesn't affect me.

BARB: That's good, Tom. Because when Jim's family tells people what you've done, and trust me they will, you won't just be hated up here, you will receive resistance the likes of which you've never seen.

TOM: Is that right?

BARB: It is. And know you what else? I'll be cheering them on.

TOM: *(Threatening tone)* Barb if you oppose me in any way know that I will do everything within my power to crush you.

BARB: *(Equally threatening tone.)* You want to go down that road? Let's do it. Otherwise get out of my face.

(A moment, then TOM *disengages. A moment where they both calm down.)*

TOM: Are you still taking regional director?

(A moment, then-)

BARB: Of course I am.

(BARB gets her bag. She heads towards the front door.)

TOM: I'm not a bad person, Barb.

BARB: I didn't say you were. People like me and Larry and your uncle, we got things to where they are now. What happens from here is on you. See you at the airport. Sir.

(BARB exits, shutting the door behind her. We hear her car start up and drive off.)

(After a beat TOM starts to get his stuff together to leave. He stops. He goes to the beds and sits on the left one. After a moment he picks up remote and turns on TV. It's static. He changes the channel. Static. Changes it and static again. He's about to change it, but he stops.)

(For several beats he watches the static.)

(Quick fade to black)

END OF PLAY